W9-CEK-438

Great Openings and Closings

Great Openings and Closings

*28 Ways to Launch and Land
Your Presentations With
Punch, Power, and Pizazz*

Mari Pat Varga

SkillPath Publications

Mission, KS

© 1996 by SkillPath Publications, a division of The Graceland College Center for Professional Development and Lifelong Learning, Inc., 6900 Squibb Road, Mission, Kansas 66202. All rights reserved. No part of this publication may be reproduced, stored in a retrieval system, or transmitted in any form by any means, electronic, mechanical, photocopying, recording, or otherwise, without the written prior permission of SkillPath Publications.

Editor: Kelly Scanlon

Copyeditor: Jenifer Dick

Page Layout: Premila Malik Borchardt and Rod Hankins

Cover Design: Rod Hankins

ISBN: 1-57294-047-6

Library of Congress Card Catalog Number: 96-67099

10   9   8   7   6   5   4   00

Printed in the United States of America

Contents

Section 1: **Great Openings**

Section 2: **Great Closings**

Introduction

Whatever kind of speaking, training, or presenting you do—whether it's a board meeting, press conference, staff get-together, speech, interview, or training session—the importance of your first and last moments with audience members is critical. Research tells us that audience members remember best what they hear first and last.

What first impression do you want to make with your audience? What is the final message you want to leave with your audience? Whether your audience is a few co-workers attending a weekly staff meeting or hundreds of conventioneers at your company's annual conference, the way you launch and land your message will determine your success.

Great Openings and Closings provides twenty-eight techniques for stimulating an audience's interest and imagination. The techniques are listed in no specific order. Choose what is most appropriate for your audience and your message. Each technique is explained, examples are given, and suggestions are provided for carrying it out. Plus, an Idea Page is provided after each technique so you can brainstorm ways to use it for future presentations. Use the page provided and keep this book handy as a workbook, or write your entries in a separate journal.

While the techniques featured in this handbook are divided into separate categories for openings and closings, keep in mind that many can be used for either. These twenty-eight tools will not only assist you in launching your presentations powerfully but will also help you land your message in a way that gives your audience a sense of closure and a call to action.

Great
Openings

Launch 1

Lift them with levity.

"We are all here for a spell, get all the good laughs you can."

—Will Rogers

Laughter brings people together. If you want to create instant rapport with your audience, lift them with levity. Humor is a great equalizer. It relieves tension and gets your audience to relax so they can listen.

You may be thinking: "Wait a second! I don't know any good jokes!" Don't fret—find the humor in the moment, in a story, or in a visual image.

But don't use humor simply for humor's sake. Be sure it illustrates a point you're trying to make.

Here are some ways you can launch your presentation with humor:

- **Relate a funny personal experience.** Chances are if it made you laugh, it will make your audience laugh.

- **If you use slides or an overhead projector, project a cartoon or amusing visual image on the screen.** You'll not only get a laugh, you'll encourage the exchange of comments among audience members.

- **Start collecting "foolish finds"**—ads in newspapers, signs in hotels and along the roadways, or the funny things people say. Then use them in your presentations when appropriate. Here are some examples:

  A road sign that reads: "You may have just passed your last exit."

  A seatback pocket airline emergency instruction card that states: "If you cannot read this card, please contact the flight attendant for further assistance."

  Shin: A device for finding furniture in the dark.

  Why is "abbreviation" such a long word?

- **If you are a good joke teller, then tell a joke.** Just be sure it's appropriate to the audience and not offensive to anyone.

- **Stretch your imagination by asking yourself "What if?"**

  What if the president of our company were Bette Midler? Colin Powell? Murphy Brown?

  What if Jim Carrey? Sam Donaldson? Madonna? headed up our sales team?

  What if we added toothpaste? insect repellent? Chia pets? to our line of products and services?

What are some of the funny scenarios you could dream up?

1. Describe what happened the last five times you laughed really hard!

2. Which of these incidents could you use to open a presentation? How?

Launch 2

Tell 'em what you're gonna tell 'em.

Have you ever delivered opening statements that were rambling or confusing? Perhaps you noticed audience members with furrowed brows, glazed-over eyes, or perplexed expressions.

Erase confusion in your listeners' minds by telling 'em what you're gonna tell 'em. State your purpose and objective simply and clearly in your opening remarks. As a presenter, you need to keep in mind that while you know where you're headed with your message, the audience usually needs guidance. Here is a quick-and-easy way to provide audience members with a "road map" to follow your message easily.

1. **Tell 'em what you are gonna tell 'em.** This is your opening.

2. **Tell 'em.** State and elaborate on your main points. These are the body of your speech.

3. **Tell 'em what you just told 'em.** This is your conclusion.

There are a number of techniques for opening your presentation by "telling 'em." Here are some examples:

- **Use alliteration.** Alliteration is the occurrence of two or more words with the same initial sound.

  The keys to great customer service are respect, rapport, and recognition. Let's first look at respect ...

- **Form an acronym with your main points.** An acronym is a word that is formed by combining the initial letters of several words.

  Tonight we will discover the A.C.T. formula to set goals. To achieve our goals, they must be achievable, concrete, and timed. Making our goals achievable provides a sound foundation...

  Don't insult your audience by being too didactic when you use this technique. For example, to say: *"Step 1 is to make your goals achievable ... Step 2 is to make your goals concrete ... and Step 3 is to make your goals timed"* may be hitting your point too hard.

- **Simply state it.** State the purpose of your presentation clearly and succinctly.

  Today, our meeting will address a five percent sales decline over the past six months.

  I want to talk to you about the pros and cons of our new computer system.

  Let's begin the morning by reviewing our performance appraisal procedures.

- **Use an abbreviation.**

    This afternoon we'll discuss the USA method for handling interruptions. The next time someone shows up unexpectedly in your office wanting to discuss something with you, offer an Understanding statement, State your own situation, and Arrange a time that's convenient for both of you to meet. Here's an example of how you can ...

Remember, the key is to let your audience know what your objective is and precisely what you will be sharing with them. You'll not only provide your audience with a road map, you'll also give yourself a mental tool for remembering your important points.

Think about your presentation. What are the main points you want to make? Experiment with capturing them in *one sentence*, using either alliteration, an acronym, or simply stating it.

Use your journal to record familiar acronyms and abbreviations that you can use to focus your main points. For example, the USA method for handling interruptions gives a familiar abbreviation a new twist, and your audience will be sure to remember it.

Launch 3

Tell a story.

You've just sat through a presentation called *The ABCs of Tiling Your Bathroom Floor*. The speaker presents a great deal of valuable information and provides an illustrated workbook. When you get home, you call a friend to report on the interesting presentation you just attended. Your friend asks for some details, but you find yourself hard pressed to remember the ABCs immediately. However, you *do* remember the humorous story the speaker told about the first time she ever attempted to tile her bathroom. *It was August of 1992 and 90 degrees outside. She was knee-deep in ceramic tile when she noticed her two children running toward her with chocolate ice cream cones melting in their hands...*

Listeners tend to remember best the stories speakers tell. These stories, personal anecdotes, and vignettes are what anchor listeners to the more complex information a speaker shares. The stories get an audience interested, hold attention, and provide reasons to listen and ways to remember the message.

You might, for example, begin a presentation on the importance of teamwork with a story about the first time you went white-water rafting with a group of people you'd never met. You could describe how you pulled together to make your daring adventure a safe one. Likewise, you might begin a presentation on the need for change within your department by sharing information about how you handled a recent job transfer, the death of a parent, or your oldest child leaving home for college.

You might be saying to yourself: "Sounds great, but I don't have any stories to tell. Nothing interesting ever happens to me!" This is a common reaction, but stories are all around you. The minute you walk out the front door in the morning you confront new people, situations, and circumstances—all of them rich with possibilities for presentation material. You need only look below the surface to unearth the message.

Begin carrying a journal with you at all times. Designate a section called "Stories to Tell." Observe everything. Be diligent about recording any event or interaction that sparks your interest. At the very least, make at least one entry each day. Here are some "seeds" from which stories might sprout:

- A conversation with a child
- An interaction with a store clerk
- Your reaction to a traffic jam
- Other people's reactions to a traffic jam
- Your response to a blue sky
- An article about a local hero
- Watching a flower bloom
- A letter from your grandmother

As you can see, the small and seemingly insignificant events and exchanges of your everyday life can be ripe with story material.

As you record the story, be sure to note each of the following. If it helps, set up your journal so that each page contains these questions.

- What happened?

- Who was involved?

- What point is illustrated?

- Where and how could you use the story?

After writing it down, speak the story into a tape recorder. Listen to it several times until you're comfortable with the way you tell it. Then, tell the story several times to different friends or co-workers. Listen to their reactions. Did they get the message you were trying to convey?

Don't take the verbal delivery of a story too casually. Look at each story as a mini-speech, and construct it with a solid opening, body, and conclusion.

Finally, use the story to open or close your next presentation.

Before your presentation, read through the "Stories to Tell" section of your journal and choose an entry that would make a good opening for your topic. Shape the story into a good strong opening. As you do, ask yourself the following questions:

- How does the story relate to my topic?

- What point(s) does it illustrate?

- Would this story appeal to this particular audience?

Launch 4

Share words of wisdom.

Most people will respond positively to a colorful, clever, concise phrase that "says it all." You can also add to your own credibility when you quote an expert, a respected authority, or a celebrity. Keep your eyes and ears open for the right person saying the right thing at the right time. Here are some great ways to find quotable material:

- **Scan books of quotes.** There are many on the market— buy several. Some of the more popular references separate quotes into topic areas such as career, love, and politics.

- **Read, read, read.** Read everything from trade publications and news journals to *People* magazine and comic strips. You never know when that magical phrase will pop up. Always carry a yellow highlighter to capture the phrase, and remind yourself later to enter it into your journal.

- **Listen, listen, listen.** The next fresh phrase you hear may be from a co-worker, neighbor, friend, or family member.

As you collect your quotes and put them to work for you, remember to avoid using overworked quotes from overexposed authorities. You may end up losing your audience's attention rather than gaining it.

Obviously, you're not going to remember everything you read or hear that strikes you as a quotable phrase. That's why it's important to note them. In your journal, start a "Words of Wisdom" section. In it, collect all the memorable phrases you've seen and heard. The only qualification for including it is that you like it. Even if you don't immediately have a specific use in mind for it, include it anyway. Weeks, months, or years later it may be the perfect quip for an occasion.

Use the following guidelines when writing your words of wisdom in your journal:

1. Record each noteworthy phrase on a fresh page in your journal.

2. Note the source.

3. Record why it strikes you as noteworthy. What point does it make?

4. Note what type of presentation it might be suited for.

Idea Page

As you design your presentation, refer often to the "Words of Wisdom" section of your journal. Note several quotes that may be appropriate for your opening. Finally, when you are finished developing your content, choose the one quote that will best set the tone for your presentation or will capture your audience's attention.

Launch 5

What's in it for them?

All eyes are on you. Your audience is thinking: "Why am I wasting my time in another meeting when I could be working on that new contract? This is such a busy time of the year. Why did they call this meeting *now?*"

You've been there. You've thought those things yourself.

Don't keep your audience guessing! Begin your presentation by telling them exactly what the benefits of listening to you are. People only listen for the benefits: they tune into station WIIFT—what's in it for them. Get on their frequency.

One word of warning: Don't presume to understand what's important to your audience. Take time to interview or survey a few audience members ahead of time to determine what they're looking for and what they value.

Ask yourself these questions when preparing your opening remarks:

- What's the value of my message to my audience?

- What will they gain by taking action on my requests?

- How will they benefit from my ideas?

- Why should they listen?

Your opening statement for a presentation skills workshop might begin in this way if you're trying to address the benefits up front:

> *"Polished presentation skills advance careers. If you want to get ahead in today's business world you must be able to speak out with confidence and clarity."*

Likewise, an opening statement for a time management seminar might be:

> *"If you want to gain two extra hours in every day, you are in the right place to learn how!"*

Or, to open a computer training class, you might say:

> *"Staying competitive in today's business marketplace is of paramount importance. This computer system will not only meet the needs of your company, it will take you one step beyond the competition."*

Idea Page

As you prepare your presentation, consider *all* the ways audience members will benefit from listening to you. Think of as many as you can—not just the obvious ones. Write them all down in a list and then go back and evaluate each one, deciding which benefit(s) you will focus on in your presentation. Finally, spend some time choosing the words you will use to convey those benefits to your audience. Be concise, but be sure that when you've finished, every member of your audience knows the answer to "What's in it for me?"

Launch 6

Be still and quiet.

Great actors know that some of their most powerful moments on stage are when they are silent. Not uttering a sound can create a memorable moment not only for the actor but for the speaker as well.

It takes an audience from five to ten seconds to take a speaker in—emotionally, mentally, and physically. Audience members begin sizing up the speaker from the moment they enter the room. Why not give the audience the opportunity to observe you without disturbance?

Here are some steps you can take to establish a positive rapport with your audience before you ever speak:

1. Walk thoughtfully to the podium or stage.

2. Make solid eye contact with a few audience members before you speak.

3. Smile a genuine smile. Let your audience know—through your facial expression and body posture—you are happy to share this time with them.

4. Breathe, pause, and only then begin to speak.

Don't confuse stillness and quiet for slow motion and dullness. You are very much alive—physically, emotionally, and mentally—in these few seconds. You're just not speaking— you're giving your audience time to take you in.

Practice being still and quiet in the following ways. Record in your journal how it felt and what you achieved by remaining quiet.

- The next time you're with a friend, allow that person to be the first to speak.

- When you're asked a question, pause deliberately and think about your answer before responding.

- After you ask a question and don't get an immediate response, wait a moment longer than you normally would before speaking.

Launch 7

Network.

People attend training seminars to gain new skills and knowledge. They also attend to meet new people and network with others in their industry who may share similar problems and concerns. It's been said that some of the best learning during a day of training takes place in the hallways and lobby.

Opening your session with a networking activity will give people an opportunity to share ideas and experiences. It also serves as an excellent "ice breaker" to loosen up the group and get everyone talking. This group activity lets your audience know that the day is going to be one of participation and audience involvement.

To open your session with a networking opportunity, assign a task to each audience member. The task should be related to the topic you'll be discussing later.

For example, you could say:

> *"Because we will be learning new skills today, I'd like to ask you to stand up, introduce yourself to three new people, and share with them one new skill you've mastered in the past three years. It might be something you once thought of as impossible but now seems easy, such as bungee cord jumping, learning a new software program, mastering the Internet, or roller blading. I'll give you five minutes. Ready, set, go!*

Here's another approach:

> *"Sharing information will be an important part of our day. To get us moving in that direction, please take three minutes now to turn to the person seated next to you, introduce yourself, describe the work you do, and share what you consider to be the most important attribute or skill for someone working in your position."*

Yet another way to create networking opportunities is to provide "name tents" for all participants. Launch your presentation by asking audience members to write their names on the front side of their tents. Then request that they use the back side of their tents for an exercise that stimulates networking. For example, you might ask them to write one of the following:

> *Three adjectives that best describe you*

> *One hobby or interest you have that might surprise others in this room*

> *A time you would consider your "personal best" when it comes to leadership in this organization*

Once participants have completed that activity, ask them to turn to their tablemates, introduce themselves, and share what they wrote down.

Any time you plan a presentation that will provide audience members with an opportunity to network, be sure to give the group clear instructions and set and state a time limit to avoid confusion and disorder.

Idea Page

In your journal, brainstorm several networking tasks and questions you could assign to break the ice and energize participants. As you consider these ideas, keep the following in mind:

- **How much time to allow for the event.** This could be affected by the total amount of time you have for your presentation, the size of the group, and/or the nature of the activity.

- **How participants will carry out the activity.** Will they be seated, standing, moving around the room? Your answer to this question will tell you such things as whether you will have enough space in the meeting room to carry out the activity, whether you'll need extra tables and chairs, pens, paper, and so on. In your journal, you might set up columns such as the following to help you organize your thoughts.

Activity	*Time Limit*	*What's Needed*
_____	_____	_____
_____	_____	_____
_____	_____	_____
_____	_____	_____

Launch 8

Give the audience "star billing."

Most people like attention, a moment in the spotlight. Consider opening your next presentation by featuring the ideas and thoughts of several members of your audience. Have the audience be the "stars" of the show.

This technique has a few obvious benefits. First, it takes the focus off you and centers it on the audience. Second, it customizes your presentation. Third, it has many humorous possibilities.

Before your next presentation, prepare a few questions you want answered. Find out the names of three or four people who will be in attendance and interview them ahead of time.

During your interviews, be sure to thoroughly explain to the interviewees how you will use their responses, and ask permission. You want to avoid embarrassing any participant. Also, make sure that everyone you interviewed plans to attend. Next, compile their answers and feature them in your opening remarks.

For example, you might say:

"We are here today to explore ways to boost our customer service ratings. But first, let's define what we mean by great customer service. Here is how some of you defined great customer service. John Jasper in Accounting said _____. *Mary Jones in Product Development said* _____. *And Bob Barnes in Telemarketing had this to say* _____ _____.*

Another way to use this technique is to ask those you interviewed to stand and report for themselves.

"As we get ready to explore a new marketing campaign for 'Super Soap,' I've asked several of you to prepare your Top Ten list of why customers should buy our product. Christine Carter, I understand you have some thoughts you'd like to tell us about..."

Yet another possibility is to send out a survey or a questionnaire to audience members prior to your presentation (see Launch 10). Use the results to create some eye-catching and stimulating graphics. One advantage to this method, particularly if the purpose of your presentation is to persuade or call the audience to action, is that you can use the results—if they're favorable—to show consensus. This may help silence nay-sayers.

One other way to give an audience "star billing" is to display something an audience member produced or use a member's accomplishment or achievement as a focal point of your presentation. For example, if your topic is the results teamwork can produce, single out the audience members who've made some noteworthy accomplishments as team members:

> *"Tom, Susan, and Chris saw their sales figures increase by 42 percent when they formed a sales team. I've asked Tom to share their success formula."*

Idea Page

As you prepare your presentation, write down questions that might yield some interesting and possibly humorous material to give your audience star billing.

For example, some suggestions for injecting humor into an awards banquet, employee recognition meeting, or retirement party might be to ask several participants what they want printed on their tombstone or what was the best advice their mother ever gave them (but didn't follow!). You might also consider favorite "sales blooper" stories.

Use your journal to record accomplishments and achievements of your colleagues, clients, and your organization as a whole. Scan the company newsletter regularly for these items. You never know when you'll be able to use one in a presentation.

Launch 9

Report research results.

Research, statistics, facts, and figures help speakers gain credibility and validate their point of view. Open your presentation with the latest research findings about the topic you'll be discussing.

Reporting research findings such as the following captures your audience's attention and provides them with an incentive to listen to the rest of your message:

For a career development talk:

> *According to the U.S. Bureau of Labor Statistics, the biggest job growth between 1990 and 2005 will occur in the following four business-related professions: information systems, marketing, management, and financial services.*

For a time management discussion:

> *To read faster and smarter, Richard Feldman, president of Learning Techniques in Merrick, N.Y., says to "read the table of contents and the first and last sentence of each paragraph in the book, and you'll get 50 percent of the ideas in most business books.*

For a sales team meeting:

*An American Management Association study done in
January indicated that 50 percent of salespeople give up
after the first call and that by the fourth call, 90 percent
have given up.*

Be sure any research you report is current, correct, and
consistent with your conclusion. If it's not, your credibility
factor will dive rather than soar.

Where do you find research results? In professional journals,
business magazines, newsletters, workshops and seminars, on-
line, and from industry experts. Here are some tips for keeping
research findings at your fingertips:

- **In your journal, start a section called "Research
  Results."** Whenever you read a statistic that interests
  you, jot it down in your journal. Be sure to note the
  source and the date.

- **Label a file or a folder "Research Results."** Clip
  articles that report or explain research findings that relate
  to your field or that might be useful some day.

To decide which research findings to begin your presentation
with, consider these questions:

- What conclusion do you want your audience to draw?

- What argument do you want to win?

- What point do you want to impress upon your audience?

- What type of research would assist you?

Idea Page

As you prepare your presentation, review your journal or file of research results. List which results would bolster your important points and would most impress the particular audience you will be facing.

If your own files don't yield any statistics or results that would drive your argument home, you may have to go find the information. Use your journal to write down what you're looking for and where you might find it.

Launch 10

Create a survey.

Create a survey containing questions that help you get to know your audience. Ask the meeting planner for permission to distribute the survey to all participants three weeks before your presentation. Compile the responses and open your presentation by revealing the results. For example:

> *"Eighteen out of twenty of you said constant policy change is the biggest challenge you currently face in your department.*

> *With seventy surveys returned, I found it fascinating that fifty-two of you cited handling customer complaints as your department's greatest strength. Even more interesting was that sixty-three of you said working in a stressful environment was your biggest challenge. Today, we'll examine where that stress is coming from..."*

Some possible survey questions you might ask are:

What does your department do well?

What accomplishment are you most proud of?

What's the biggest challenge you currently face?

How would you describe the future of your industry?

Where do you see possibilities for growth in this company?

The information you gather from your survey will be a valuable asset in custom designing your presentation and providing your audience with a "snapshot" of fellow employee attitudes and opinions. A survey also allows your audience to feel they actively participated in setting the agenda for the presentation.

You may get information you don't expect. For instance, you may discover company morale is at an all-time low despite assurances otherwise. Once you ask people to complete the survey, be prepared to reveal the results—good or bad. Your participants will expect it.

Idea Page

As you prepare your presentation, write down anything you'd like to know about your audience—their feelings and opinions, what's going on in their jobs, and so on—that would help you to customize your presentation or to reinforce your points with that particular audience. For example, if you're trying to sell them on the possibilities of future growth, and the survey results reveal the company's just been through a downsizing, that would be valuable information to have.

In addition, keep in mind that the format of your survey has a lot to do with the quality of the responses you receive. Word your questions clearly and succinctly, and encourage comments. Avoid questions that can be answered "yes" or "no" or "True" or "False." These types of closed questions discourage thoughtful responses.

Launch 11

What's in the news?

Every day in every newspaper across the country are stories—big and small—that may provide you with the perfect opening for your next presentation. Begin your next talk by tying your topic to a current event.

This technique works best if you work backwards. Write and design your presentation first. Be clear about your objective, theme, and purpose. Then begin to look for newsworthy items that might create a powerful opening. Ask yourself: What is the theme of my presentation? What is my core message?

Next, look for a news story or local event that might illustrate your central theme. Examine stories you hear on the evening news or read about in the morning paper in the same way you would a personal anecdote. Determine whether to use a particular news story by asking yourself:

- What's the point?

- What does this story illustrate?

- Does telling this story serve my presentation's purpose?

Be cautious of using a local event that may be too tragic or sensitive to the audience. Be confident they are ready to listen to a reference to the event.

Idea Page

Read your local newspaper cover to cover for one week. Cut out articles related to the themes or core messages of the presentations you usually give. Paste the articles in your journal.

This will get you in the habit of using the news as a possible source for opening your presentations. After one week, you should be accustomed to clipping these items and continue to do so automatically. Other sources for timely news events are magazines, television and radio newscasts, and on-line news services. Then, when you prepare your presentations, you'll have a variety of articles to choose from.

Launch 12

Tell a heroic story.

Inspire your audience by opening your presentation with a hero's story. Too often the bad news—violence, poverty, drugs, and disease—snatch top billing. Audiences are hungry for stories with a positive message. If you want to encourage, excite, or energize your audience members to peak performance levels, spur them on with a memorable story of heroism.

Heroic men and women are everywhere. Some are commonly noted: athletes, astronauts, and artists. Some have names most would recognize; others may be known to few people outside their neighborhood. Look for heroes in newspapers and magazines, on television, in your community, within your family, and within yourself.

What lessons do the following examples of heroism teach?

British mountaineer Alison Hargreaves became the first woman to ever reach the summit of Mount Everest. She did the climb alone and without using oxygen tanks. While she died in August 1995 trying to scale the world's second largest mountain, Pakistan's K2, she leaves behind the memories of a life dedicated to adventure and risk taking. Alison lived and died by her favorite saying: "One day as a tiger is better than a thousand as a sheep."

South Bronx teenager Gil C. Alicea rose above his drug and violence-ridden environment and tragic family circumstances to write a memoir entitled, The Air Down Here: True Tales From a South Bronx Boyhood. *This young man's story is a moving testimony to the resilience of children.*

When baseball legend Cal Ripken, Jr., was praised for breaking Lou Gehrig's record of playing in 2,130 consecutive games, he brushed off the accolades and instead praised America's real working heroes. One of the heroes he cited was Mildred Parsons, 82, who hasn't missed a day of work as a secretary for the Federal Bureau of Investigation in fifty-six years! Her streak started in 1939.

Telling a story about heroism works best for speeches or presentations meant to inspire and motivate. Be cautious not to overexaggerate any person's accomplishments. Let their own story be the message. Avoid manipulating your audience's emotions.

When searching for a hero's story, ask yourself these questions to determine the story's merit and whether it helps to illustrate your point:

- What is the core message of this person's story?

- Does that message match my presentation's purpose?

- Who was this person before his or her heroic venture?

- What obstacles did the person overcome?

- What was the person's conflict?

- What was the climax?

- Who did the person become as a result of the heroic journey?

- What can be learned from this person's experience?

Label a section in your journal "Heroic Tales." Every time you hear of someone whose behavior or actions elevate them to hero status, record the details in your journal. Also write down why you think the person is a hero. Don't overlook "silent" heroes, the people who persevere through hardships or make sacrifices so someone else's life can be better.

Launch 13

Mingle, mingle, mingle.

Your presentation actually begins the minute you enter the room. Audience members watch you with interest and wonder what you will say when the formal program begins.

Mingling with individual audience members before your presentation gives you an edge in establishing rapport and camaraderie with the audience. When you begin your presentation, your audience is already comfortable and familiar with you.

Prepare for your pre-presentation mingling by having some specific questions in mind, particularly questions that relate to the topic you'll be addressing:

What is the most important thing you came here to learn today?

What are the biggest challenges you now face in your community?

What is your most difficult obstacle in obtaining and retaining volunteers?

Note that these are open-ended questions requiring more than a "yes" or "no" answer.

Your formal presentation might begin like this:

"O.K., it's now time to begin our workshop. While talking with many of you, I gathered that the one question you most want answered today is, How do we handle our increased workload without having to add hours to our workday? Since so many of you are interested in that situation, let's go ahead and examine it first."

If you plan to use a statement or comment someone made to you privately, be sure to ask permission to state it publicly.

Another approach you can take in your pre-presentation mingling is to share information about yourself. You might, for example, offer information about your background or experience with the topic to be discussed. When appropriate, you might offer personal details such as a description of your family, where you're from, and so on—anything to make you "real" to your audience. This approach, of course, encourages audience members to do the same. Then you can begin your presentation with comments like:

"Well, it looks like I've got quite a few fellow Southerners in the room today..."

"Now that some of us have decided a trip to the Carribean would be our favorite winter get-away, let's switch from fantasy to reality and talk about..."

Idea Page

In your journal, list several questions you might ask as you mingle with your audience before beginning your presentation. After each presentation, note which ones generated the most response and created the greatest rapport. If a question you asked received a lukewarm reaction, note that too. Try rewording it and use it again. Or perhaps it just wasn't the right question to ask that particular audience. Try it on a different group.

Practice sharing personal information with your audience. What are you comfortable discussing? Note your audience's reaction. Did the stories about your children get a positive response? How about your spouse's cooking skills?

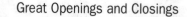

Launch 14

Let your audience decide the direction.

At times, you may find yourself in a situation in which you'll need to customize your presentation on the spot. You may be presenting to a group you've never met and for whom you have no background information. Or you may have four hours worth of information to share, but at the last minute be told you have only one hour in which to present it.

What do you do?

Open your presentation by asking the audience what direction they want the presentation to take. Use either a flip chart (for small groups under thirty people) or a blank overhead transparency on a projector (for larger groups) to collect information about the group's needs and interests.

Sample questions to ask might be:

What are the most important skills you want to gain today?

There's a lot we could cover today. What do you think would be most valuable?

After you have received a fair amount of responses, look for consensus:

It looks like a majority of you want to discuss whether or not this new computer system will really benefit our customer service standards. I'll now share with you how it will accomplish that goal.

Let's see a show of hands—how many of you want to talk about how to increase sales?

Dealing with difficult customers got a reaction from many of you—raise your hand if that is an area you want covered today.

Am I reading you correctly? How many of you want to discuss time management?

A word of warning: Use this technique only if you are willing to toss out the outline. In other words, feel confident in your level of expertise and knowledge of your topic. Be prepared for your audience to take you in an unexpected and unrehearsed direction.

Idea Page

The best way to prepare yourself to speak at a moment's notice or to change your presentation on the spot is to be proactive. *Expect* that someday you'll find yourself in just such a situation, and take steps now to confront it. First, list all the possible areas of interest your audience members might have in the topics you typically speak on. Next, gauge your comfort level in discussing those areas. Finally, prepare yourself to speak credibly and confidently in any of the areas you pinpointed. Identify the areas you feel are your weak points and find the information you need to speak knowledgeably.

2

Great Closings

Landing **1**

Tell 'em what you told 'em.

A well-organized presentation often follows this time-tested structure:

- Tell 'em what you are going to tell 'em.

- Tell 'em.

- Tell 'em what you just told 'em.

Closing your presentation using this design (refer back to Launch 2 for details on how to begin your presentation using this structure) refreshes your audience's memory of what you've covered and reminds them of what they need to take action on.

For example, you might conclude your presentation by carrying through on an alliteration device you introduced early in your presentation:

So, remember the next time you're face to face with an angry customer, use the three Rs of customer service excellence: Responsiveness, Respect, and Rapport.

Or just simply sum up your presentation by repeating your key points:

When you begin your day tomorrow, keep in mind what we've discussed today—the value of scheduling your priorities, determining what is most important to you, and keeping your personal mission in mind.

Just be sure your conclusion is directly tied to your opening. In other words, your conclusion should be the mirror image of your opening remarks. Make sure your conclusion tells 'em what you promised you'd tell 'em!

Idea Page

After preparing your presentation, review your key points and write several concluding statements that sum up what you promised your audience you'd tell 'em. Which flow best? Which are most powerful?

To determine the concluding remarks you like best, say them out loud—to yourself, the living room furniture, a friend, your cat or dog. The idea is to become so comfortable with your words that they sound conversational—not formal and stilted. You might even record your conclusion (or entire presentation) and listen to it while cleaning the house or driving to work so you become familiar and relaxed with it. This also helps you detect problem or awkward areas.

Experiment with various ways of reminding your audience what you told 'em:

- Write the key points on a flip chart or overhead transparency.

- Create a slide with interesting graphics that restate your main points.

- Ask audience members to recall your key points—offer prizes or incentives for those who volunteer.

- If you've used an acronym (S.T.R.I.V.E. for Success), consider putting it on bumper stickers, bookmarks, or buttons and distributing them.

Landing 2

Do a benefit review.

This closing technique is an extension of Launch 5—What's in It for Them?—which suggests explaining upfront why your audience should listen to you. Now, close your presentation powerfully by reviewing those benefits.

The following two examples illustrate how to do so effectively:

"As I mentioned at the beginning of our day, polished presentation skills are a brilliant way to increase your visibility, gain marketing opportunities, and receive a professional promotion. Be diligent and continue to work on the techniques we discussed today, and you will be successful."

"Remember, by matching your customer's vocal pitch, rhythm, and speed, you'll win their trust, loyalty, and their business!"

Be sure that what you perceive as the benefits of your presentation are ones you are confident will appeal to and have value to your audience.

Perfect this concluding technique by confirming you are communicating benefits clearly. Rehearse your entire presentation in front of friends, family, or professional colleagues (or put your presentation on tape and have them listen at their convenience). Later, ask what motivated them to listen. In other words, what benefits did they perceive in your message? Once you're confident you've clearly established what's in it for them, your benefit review will flow naturally.

Practice different ways to review benefits:

- Ask your audience how your information will help them—write all responses on a flip chart.

- Break the audience into small groups and ask them to brainstorm a list of benefits.

Landing 3

Ask a question.

Your conclusion should leave your audience with something to think about. Asking a rhetorical question that captures the purpose of your speech will give your audience something to consider.

> *Our discussion on the importance of a positive attitude begs me to leave you with one question to think over: Would your company be a better place to work if everyone followed your example?*

> *Considering the facts we've presented here tonight, are you willing to walk away from this meeting without voting "yes" on this petition for your children's safety? ... Which leads me to ask, are you part of the problem or part of the solution?*

As you consider this type of closing, keep your topic—and the mood of your audience—in mind. Remember that each audience is different. A closing question that hits home with one audience might leave another audience thinking that you're simply playing with their emotions.

When concluding with a question, conclude. Don't diminish the power of a single, purposeful question by adding additional thoughts. Ask it, pause, and leave the stage.

Browse magazine and newspaper ads and observe the way advertisers attempt to grab reader attention with a single question. Notice what questions are most persuasive in getting consumers to buy.

Are you smart enough to stay ahead of the competition?

Can you afford NOT to use Sparkle toothpaste?

When was the last time you had this much fun...in a car?

If all video cameras are the same, why did one win twenty-five major awards last year?

Remember, you're trying to "sell" your ideas just as advertisers are attempting to sell their products. Imagine you're writing an ad for your presentation's central message. What provocative or poignant question might you pose that would leave your audience wanting more?

Landing 4

Follow a circular construction.

Read any good books lately? Think for a moment about some of the great novels you've read. Many good authors begin with a captivating image, tell the story, and conclude with the same image they began with. Learn to speak the way good writers write.

This technique is a powerful way to conclude a presentation. There are a couple of clear benefits. First, if you've come up with an opening you love, you automatically have the foundation for a splendid close. Second, you give your audience a sense of closure and completion.

For example, you might open a presentation on stress management in this way:

> *My daughter came to me last week and asked if I'd join her and her friends jumping rope outside. I smiled, but eager to get back to my work, I hurriedly responded, "Honey, thanks for asking, but I'm too busy right now to jump rope." She paused for a moment, looked me straight in the eye, and said: "That's why I'm asking, Mom. You need to get out and play!"*

I will share with you today, how I've learned to deal with stress by making more time for play...

You can close that same presentation with this powerful conclusion:

So the next time you're feeling overwhelmed, overburdened, and stressed-out—take a little time out to play. Get in touch with the child in you. I can assure you that now when I get an invitation from my daughter to jump rope, I race her out the door!

Be sure the image or anecdote you're using is both accessible and meaningful to your audience. It should be something they can immediately identify with. Circular construction is the foundation your entire presentation is built on—be sure it's a solid one.

Idea Page

The next time one of your presentations lends itself to a circular construction, get visual. Actually draw a circle in your journal and plot the points of your presentation on that model. This will provide a graphical representation of your presentation, and you'll be able to see at a glance the progression of your ideas as the ending ties back up with the beginning. As you plot the points you've developed, note any that don't add to the progression. These are your weak points. Plot them outside the circle as a reminder to strengthen them—or eliminate them altogether.

Landing 5

Use illuminating images.

Consider concluding your next presentation with a single image (one you can display on an overhead or slide projector). The image you choose—a photograph, cartoon, illustration—should summarize your message and be strong enough to stand alone without explanation.

A Gary Larsen (*The Far Side*) cartoon, for example, might be the perfect way to end a presentation about looking at the humor in everyday life. Photographs of participants pursuing their personal hobbies (gardening, horseback riding, roller blading, or parenting) would be a perfect conclusion to a discussion about the importance of balance in our lives. A slide showing the company's new mission statement could provide a powerful reminder of goals.

Be aware that you can't reproduce and distribute to audience members any copyrighted image without getting permission from the author, creator, or copyright holder.

Some possible sources of thought-provoking images include the following:

- The Sunday comics or books of cartoons
- Magazines
- Contributions from your audience (photographs)
- Clip art collections
- Your own photographs

Idea page

Create file folders labeled with the titles of the topics you usually present on (e.g., team building, stress management, etc.). When you see an image that is appropriate to one of these topics, put it in the folder for consideration. When you're struggling to find the perfect conclusion, leaf through the folder. Even if you don't find the right image every time, one of the items you clipped may inspire another type of conclusion.

Landing 6

Play a theme song.

Is there a piece of music that embodies your message or mission? Use music to end your presentation on a high note. Music is a powerful way to bring people together, influence the pace, set the tone, and inspire them to action.

Likewise, speakers can influence their audiences with music. A travel agent promoting vacations to the Caribbean might conclude her talk with a few minutes of Calypso music, for example.

Keep in mind that the music you select may fall under the jurisdiction of various licensing agencies that protect the distribution of copyrighted music. If you are making a profit from your event, you may need to pay a user fee to a licensing agency such as BMI or ASCAP. Many presenters use music they have purchased, not realizing a performance fee is due any time the music is played. Other alternatives are to contract original music or use copyright fee paid music.

Idea Page

In your journal, write down the names of musical pieces that move you in some way—whether they inspire you, energize you, sadden you, and so on. Do this regularly. Be sure to record how you felt when you heard the song and what affect it had on your mood. Then jot down what types of presentations would be enhanced by the song. Later, when you're searching for just the right song to create a mood for your presentation, consult your journal.

Landing 7

Call for commitment.

You've excited your audience about your ideas. You've persuaded them to see things your way. Now what? People often need an extra push or invitation to take the ideas they've learned and act on them.

When preparing your presentation, write your objective on a sticky note and post it where you can see it as you're writing. Keep your objective simple:

The purpose of my presentation is to

_____.

After my presentation, my audience will

_____.

Keeping the purpose of your presentation in mind will keep you focused while you're preparing your presentation. A clear and concise conclusion will flow naturally from the body of your presentation.

Consider how a presentation with this objective might conclude:

The purpose of my presentation is to convince my students of the competitive advantage of doing research on-line.

After my presentation, my students will head straight to the library and begin exploring on-line capabilities.

The speaker closed the presentation in this way:

Now that you're aware of the competitive advantages of tapping into the limitless information available on-line, run—don't walk—to the library to begin your research now. Be committed to excellence. Get on-line today!

One way to encourage your audience to take action immediately is to have support material ready at the end of your presentation:

- A petition ready to sign

- A product ready for purchase

- Discounts available only *today!*

- Reference sheets with phone numbers and addresses

Just make sure that when you're calling for commitment from your audience, you've already made the commitment yourself. Don't ask your listeners to do something you aren't willing or able to do. In other words, don't ask them to commit to living a more balanced lifestyle when you haven't achieved that goal yourself.

In order to call for a commitment, you have to convince your audience of WIIFM (Launch 5) and remind them of the benefits (Landing 2). So, practice writing out the benefits of committing to your plan of action and work them into your call for commitment closing. Notice that in the example on page 69, that the implied benefit is staying one step ahead of the competition.

Landing 8

Dream of the possibilities.

Conclude your next presentation by creating a "dream scene" of what it would be like if your audience made good use of your ideas and suggestions. Paint a word picture to help them visualize success.

Here's how one speaker concluded a workshop on presentation skills:

> *"Imagine for a moment that you are about to make an important business presentation. You came up with an exciting idea that you're dying to share. You've practiced in front of the mirror several times and have eliminated nervous gestures. Your pace, message, and gestures are now working in sync. You feel comfortable and confident. You enter the boardroom and find it filled with smiling, friendly faces.*
>
> *After hearing your presentation, your colleagues seem fired up and your boss requests that you give her an action plan by the end of the week explaining how you would implement your idea.*
>
> *Good luck on your next presentation!"*

Don't hurry or minimize the power of this conclusion. This technique requires a bit of dramatic flair. Be willing to do what it takes to create the atmosphere (e.g., dimming the lights, creating a poetic pause, requesting the audience members to close their eyes).

Idea Page

As you prepare your presentation, describe in detail what it would be like if your audience took your ideas and suggestions and made them a reality. Think of all the possibilities. Then take your rough draft and polish it, adding notes to yourself about when to pause and where to add emphasis. Also consider what devices you will use to create the right atmosphere. Will you use music? dim the lights? ask audience members to close their eyes? Try to involve sensory perception in your description. Ask your audience to imagine a certain scene, hear a certain sound (e.g., applause, cheers), and so on. Finally, practice your delivery. You might ask a friend or family member to listen to you to see whether you actually create the reaction you're striving for.

Landing 9

Build buddy pacts.

Use the buddy system to encourage audience members to implement the ideas you discuss during your presentation. Simply assign each participant a "buddy" they are accountable to. Have the pair establish goals, exchange telephone numbers, and decide on a contact date. On that predetermined date, the buddies will call one another to check on the progress they've made and the obstacles they've encountered.

Here's how you can present the idea:

Our goal this year is to raise $100,000 through our silent auction. The first step is to obtain great auction items. We'd like to see each committee member bring in ten items valued at more than $100 each. Support and encouragement are important factors in achieving this challenging goal. Please choose a buddy, exchange telephone numbers, and plan to contact this person on April 17 and May 10 to report your progress and brainstorm solutions to problems. Working together, we can make this event a success!

This technique can easily fail if you don't give audience members a simple way to follow through with your request. Make it easy for them by distributing colored index cards they can quickly fill out and exchange (see accompanying example). Preprint the cards and design them to fit your needs. You might also create a goal-setting worksheet that buddies can use to measure progress.

Sample Index Card

Buddy's name: _____

Telephone number: _____

Goal: _____

Call date: _____

Idea Page

Brainstorm as many ideas as you can to implement a "buddy pact" to help individuals achieve their goals. What devices besides the index card and goal-setting worksheet might work for your particular group? Perhaps holding periodic strategy sessions, or offering incentives for the "buddy" team that's first to reach its goal would be effective. Jot your ideas in your journal as you think of them.

Landing 10

Ink ideas.

Many participants feel overwhelmed at the end of a day of training. Flooded with many new ideas, participants walk away bewildered and confused about which to take action on first. Simplify the process for them by concluding your day with an activity called "inked ideas."

At the end of your session, ask people to take a few minutes to write down what they consider to be the best ideas they heard during the day. As the expression goes, "When you think it, ink it." Ask your participants to commit their ideas to paper.

For example:

> We've discussed many different ways to improve your sales performance today. To help you focus on which ideas would be most beneficial for you, take a moment now to write down the top three ideas you plan to take action on when you leave here this afternoon. I'll give you five minutes to complete this exercise.

Consider asking several volunteers to relate their top three ideas to the group. As an incentive and to add humor, offer special ink pens or light bulbs (representing great ideas) to those who volunteer. Asking for volunteers to report helps reinforce ideas introduced during the day's training and stimulates the thinking of those who might be stuck.

Be prepared for the possibility that audience members might find it difficult to come up with individual ideas on the spur of the moment. They may already be on overload. Ready yourself for some on-the-spot coaching. For instance, ask:

What was the best benefit statement you heard?

Did the discussion on "relationship" selling have an impact on you?

What technique could you imagine using?

What is the best time of the day to make a follow-up call?

Idea Page

For your next training day, prepare a special page to add to your handouts. Title this page "Inked Ideas."

Be sure to compose a list of your top ideas of the day. It may come in handy if participants need help.

Another idea is to place several flip charts around the meeting room. Title them "I Need Ideas." Encourage participants to grab a marker and write down their favorite ideas as they hear them throughout the day (preferably during breaks).

Conclude the day by simply reviewing what's written on the flip charts.

Landing 11

Share intentions.

Conclude your meeting by having participants share what they intend to do with the information they learned. Simply ask participants to break into small groups and share what they intend to do with the knowledge they gained throughout the day. You can ask them to use the following questions as guidelines for their discussion:

What do I intend to do?

What do I intend to stop doing?

What do I intend to continue doing?

What do I intend to teach to a co-worker or friend?

If you choose to conclude your presentation by asking participants to share their intentions, consider the following factors:

- Size of groups

- Materials the groups may need

- Time frame allowed

- Who will report for each group (optional)

Don't rush this exercise. You may want to give participants a few minutes on their own to formulate their ideas before they discuss them in a group setting.

Idea Page

As you prepare your presentation, anticipate that some participants may have some trouble immediately thinking of how they will implement what they learned. Ask them to think of a specific situation they are currently involved with that relates to your topic. Then review each of your points and ask the person to relate each point to that situation.

Landing 12

Provide conclusion cues.

Signal the end of your presentation by using "conclusion cues." These phrases help focus audience attention. They also quiet a restless audience and wake up inattentive participants.

Some examples of conclusion cues:

And so, what has today really been about? First . . .

Now, in conclusion . . .

Bringing it all together, let me remind you . . .

One last thought that summarizes our agenda today . . .

Finally . . .

When you say you're going to conclude—conclude. Don't use your conclusion as an opportunity to introduce new ideas and concepts. Once people hear "in conclusion," they count on the meeting to end in a few minutes. Audiences don't forgive speakers who don't deliver what they promise!

In your journal, brainstorm a list of conclusion cues. Keep them handy as you prepare your presentations. You'll also find the list invaluable if you have to speak on the spur of the moment.

Landing 13

Stop with shock.

Jolt your audience by concluding your speech with an unusual fact or provocative statement. Leave them slightly off-center and struggling to regain balance as they leave the room. This technique will get your audience thinking and talking about your presentation long after they've left the building.

Shocking remarks can take these forms:

- A question
- An unusual fact
- A historical event
- Current news
- A quotation
- A strong opinion
- A visual image

Here are some examples:

If you don't switch to this new technology to increase sales, your company will be out of business by the end of next year.

Author Harvey McKay says that anyone who graduates from college never having taken a speech course should be classified a bum. I couldn't agree more. You'd be foolish not to work diligently on the presentation skills we've discussed here today.

As Tom Peters says, "It's an insane world, and in an insane world, sane organizations make no sense." We must begin today to do things differently than we've ever done them before.

An image consultant showing dramatic "before and after" photographs of client make-overs.

A nutritionist displaying a model of what three pounds of fat really looks like!

Be aware that a few members of your audience might be offended by your no-holds barred conclusion. Tell the truth and be ready to accept the consequences of your comments. Make sure you're comfortable with the message. State it with confidence and conviction. Make no excuses. Be bold and make it count!

Idea Page

For a conclusion intended to shock your audience, you might find the journal entries and files you've created for statistics, quotes, and anecdotes helpful.

Practice writing bold statements and rehearsing out loud until you think they provide just the jolt you're trying to achieve.

Landing 14

Leave 'em crying.

Ever heard the old expression "start 'em laughing and leave 'em crying"? The message here is to begin your presentation with humor but end it on a poignant, thoughtful note. Change the pace and close your presentation with the inspirational lyrics to a song, a children's fairy tale, a poem, or a bit of prose.

Do you have a favorite story or poem that lifts your spirits every time you read it? Chances are, if it has that effect on you, it will have the same effect on your audience.

When it comes time to conclude, let your audience know you have something special to share.

"I'd like to take a moment now to share the thoughts of my favorite philosopher, 'The Cat in the Hat' ... "

"We've talked today about valuing each team member. These sentiments are best expressed in the lyrics of a favorite song of mine. Let me share those with you now."

At this point, bring out the book or piece of paper where you've written the words. You may want to make the moment a bit more dramatic by pulling out a stool to sit on or moving closer to the center of the room. Allow this to be an intimate moment with your group.

Remember, you can't reprint the copyrighted materials of others without their permission.

Idea Page

Use your journal to write down specific passages in books, poems, or songs that are meaningful to you. When you're in need of a poignant closing, look no further than your journal.

Don't overlook the power of a real-life story either. If you read about a particularly poignant situation, or experience one first-hand, write it down in your journal. Children are often a good source of this type of material, for they aren't embarrassed to express their true feelings.

Bibliography and Suggested Reading

Allen, Jeffrey G. *The Career Trap: Breaking Through the 10 Year Barrier to Get the Job You Really Want.* New York: AMACOM Books, 1995.

Anderson, Peggy. *Great Quotes from Great Leaders.* Lombard, IL: Great Quotations Publishing Company, 1990.

Cameron, Julia-Bryan, Mark. *The Artist's Way.* New York: Putnam, 1992.

Decker, Bert. *You've Got to be Believed to be Heard.* New York: St. Martin's Press, 1992.

Peters, Tom. *The Tom Peters Seminar: Crazy Times Call for Crazy Organizations.* New York: Vintage Books, 1994.

Pike, Robert W. *Creative Training Techniques Handbook.* Minneapolis, MN: Lakewood Books, 1989.

Scannell, Edward, and John Newstrom. *Games Trainers Play.* New York: McGraw-Hill, 1991.

Walters, Lilly. *What to Say When...You're Dying on the Platform.* New York: McGraw-Hill, 1991.

Available From SkillPath Publications

Self-Study Sourcebooks

Climbing the Corporate Ladder: What You Need to Know and Do to Be a Promotable Person *by Barbara Pachter and Marjorie Brody*

Coping With Supervisory Nightmares: 12 Common Nightmares of Leadership and What You Can Do About Them *by Michael and Deborah Singer Dobson*

Defeating Procrastination: 52 Fail-Safe Tips for Keeping Time on Your Side *by Marlene Caroselli, Ed.D.*

Discovering Your Purpose *by Ivy Haley*

Going for the Gold: Winning the Gold Medal for Financial Independence *by Lesley D. Bissett, CFP*

Having Something to Say When You Have to Say Something: The Art of Organizing Your Presentation *by Randy Horn*

Info-Flood: How to Swim in a Sea of Information Without Going Under *by Marlene Caroselli, Ed.D.*

The Innovative Secretary *by Marlene Caroselli, Ed.D.*

Letters & Memos: Just Like That! *by Dave Davies*

Mastering the Art of Communication: Your Keys to Developing a More Effective Personal Style *by Michelle Fairfield Poley*

Organized for Success! 95 Tips for Taking Control of Your Time, Your Space, and Your Life *by Nanci McGraw*

A Passion to Lead! How to Develop Your Natural Leadership Ability *by Michael Plumstead*

P.E.R.S.U.A.D.E.: Communication Strategies That Move People to Action *by Marlene Caroselli, Ed.D.*

Productivity Power: 250 Great Ideas for Being More Productive *by Jim Temme*

Promoting Yourself: 50 Ways to Increase Your Prestige, Power, and Paycheck *by Marlene Caroselli, Ed.D.*

Proof Positive: How to Find Errors Before They Embarrass You *by Karen L. Anderson*

Risk-Taking: 50 Ways to Turn Risks Into Rewards *by Marlene Caroselli, Ed.D. and David Harris*

Speak Up and Stand Out: How to Make Effective Presentations *by Nanci McGraw*

Stress Control: How You Can Find Relief From Life's Daily Stress *by Steve Bell*

The Technical Writer's Guide *by Robert McGraw*

Total Quality Customer Service: How to Make It Your Way of Life *by Jim Temme*

Write It Right! A Guide for Clear and Correct Writing *by Richard Andersen and Helene Hinis*

Your Total Communication Image *by Janet Signe Olson, Ph.D.*

Handbooks

The ABC's of Empowered Teams: Building Blocks for Success *by Mark Towers*

Assert Yourself! Developing Power-Packed Communication Skills to Make Your Points Clearly, Confidently, and Persuasively *by Lisa Contini*

Breaking the Ice: How to Improve Your On-the-Spot Communication Skills
by Deborah Shouse

The Care and Keeping of Customers: A Treasury of Facts, Tips, and Proven
Techniques for Keeping Your Customers Coming BACK! *by Roy Lantz*

Challenging Change: Five Steps for Dealing With Change *by Holly DeForest and
Mary Steinberg*

Dynamic Delegation: A Manager's Guide for Active Empowerment *by Mark Towers*

Every Woman's Guide to Career Success *by Denise M. Dudley*

Grammar? No Problem! *by Dave Davies*

Great Openings and Closings: 28 Ways to Launch and Land Your Presentations With
Punch, Power, and Pizazz *by Mari Pat Varga*

Hiring and Firing: What Every Manager Needs to Know *by Marlene Caroselli, Ed.D.
with Laura Wyeth, Ms.Ed.*

How to Be a More Effective Group Communicator: Finding Your Role and Boosting
Your Confidence in Group Situations *by Deborah Shouse*

How to Deal With Difficult People *by Paul Friedman*

Learning to Laugh at Work: The Power of Humor in the Workplace
by Robert McGraw

Making Your Mark: How to Develop a Personal Marketing Plan for Becoming More
Visible and More Appreciated at Work *by Deborah Shouse*

Meetings That Work *by Marlene Caroselli, Ed.D.*

The Mentoring Advantage: How to Help Your Career Soar to New Heights
by Pam Grout

Minding Your Business Manners: Etiquette Tips for Presenting Yourself
Professionally in Every Business Situation *by Marjorie Brody and Barbara Pachter*

Misspeller's Guide *by Joel and Ruth Schroeder*

Motivation in the Workplace: How to Motivate Workers to Peak Performance and
Productivity *by Barbara Fielder*

NameTags Plus: Games You Can Play When People Don't Know What to Say
by Deborah Shouse

Networking: How to Creatively Tap Your People Resources *by Colleen Clarke*

New & Improved! 25 Ways to Be More Creative and More Effective *by Pam Grout*

Power Write! A Practical Guide to Words That Work *by Helene Hinis*

The Power of Positivity: Eighty ways to energize your life
by Joel and Ruth Schroeder

Putting Anger to Work For You *by Ruth and Joel Schroeder*

Reinventing Your Self: 28 Strategies for Coping With Change *by Mark Towers*

Saying "No" to Negativity: How to Manage Negativity in Yourself, Your Boss, and
Your Co-Workers *by Zoie Kaye*

The Supervisor's Guide: The Everyday Guide to Coordinating People and Tasks
by Jerry Brown and Denise Dudley, Ph.D.

Taking Charge: A Personal Guide to Managing Projects and Priorities
by Michal E. Feder

Treasure Hunt: 10 Stepping Stones to a New and More Confident You! *by Pam Grout*

A Winning Attitude: How to Develop Your Most Important Asset!
by Michelle Fairfield Poley

For more information, call 1-800-873-7545.